YEAR 2

GRAMMAR AND PUNCTUATION

Do you need to know the basics of punctuation and grammar? Let's read together and learn...

Parents and carers are encouraged to read the explanation and practice sections with their child.

Victoria Hazell

Illustrated by Janice Bowles

About this book

This book is designed to review the essential Grammar and Punctuation skills required in Year 2.

Each unit begins with a brief **explanation** of a particular grammar or punctuation concept. This is followed by examples of how this concept is used in text **(We practise)**. Parents or carers are encouraged to read the explanation and the **We practise** section together with their child.

Practical exercises are then provided to give your child the opportunity to practise the concept **(You practise)**. These exercises reinforce the concept and check that your child understands it fully.

The four **tests** at the back of the book can be done once the book has been completed. These are designed to check that your child's punctuation and grammar skills are consolidated.

If further instruction is required, we recommend that this book be provided to your child's teacher for review. Then the parent or carer and the teacher can devise a plan to ensure all the basic concepts are fully understood and consolidated.

Meet 'BOB' – Back Of the Book

At the end of each unit, BOB reminds your child to go to the **Answer** section at the Back of the Book to check the answers.

Victoria Hazell

Game Card Instructions

Parts of speech

Remove and cut out the cards and then sort the words to match the six parts of speech in red: nouns, adjectives, verbs, pronouns, conjunctions and adverbs.

Australian Curriculum Year 2

Text structure & organisation

Understand how texts are made cohesive through resources, for example word associations, synonyms, and antonyms (ACELA1464)

Recognise that capital letters signal proper nouns and commas are used to separate items in lists (ACELA1465)

Expressing & developing ideas

Understand that simple connections can be made between ideas by using a compound sentence with two or more clauses and coordinating conjunctions (ACELA1467)

Understand that nouns represent people, places, things and ideas and can be, for example, common, proper, concrete and abstract, and that noun groups can be expanded using articles and adjectives (ACELA1468)

Recognise common prefixes and suffixes and how they change a word's meaning (ACELA1472)

Contents & Checklist

CAPITAL LETTERS

Capital letter A letter written in upper case, or a 'big' letter. **A** is the capital letter for **a**.

A capital letter is used for the first word of a **new sentence**.

Capital letters are also used for **proper nouns**. A **noun** is the name of a person, place or thing. A proper noun is the name of a particular person or a special place or thing. Proper nouns start with a capital letter to show that they are important.

Important names begin with a capital letter.

Once upon a time there was an ogre named Shrek and he married Princess Fiona.

We practise

The capital letters are underlined in each sentence.

My family lives in Australia.
Proper noun = **Australia** is the name of an important place
My is the start of a **new sentence**

You can buy fruit from Harry's Fruit Shop.
Proper noun = **Harry's Fruit Shop** is the name of a particular place
You is the start of a **new sentence**

Your birthday is in May.
Proper noun = **May** is the name of a month of the year
Your is the start of a **new sentence**

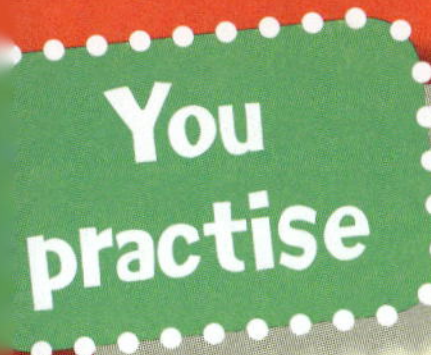

Underline the letters that should be capital letters in each sentence.

Hint: The number in brackets tells you the number of capital letters.

1. today is monday and it is a school day. (2)

2. watch out for that truck! (1)

3. have you seen the movie called *shrek*? (2)

4. mr walker is our teacher at school this year. (2)

5. our dog ben carried the ball in his mouth. (2)

BOB time!

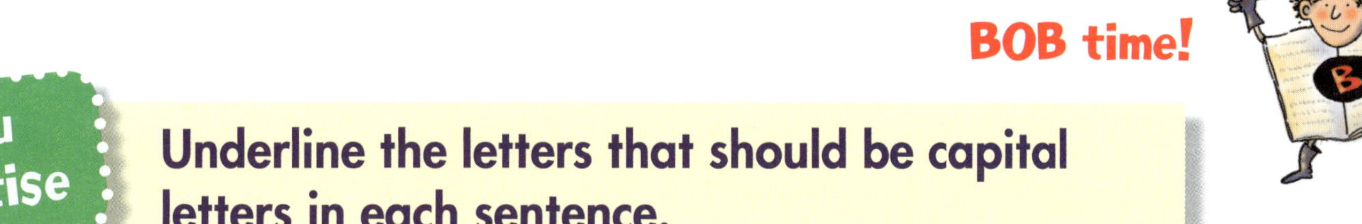

6. on saturdays tim loves to watch the football. (3)

7. my friends sophie and anna are coming for a sleepover. (3)

8. we went on a holiday to queensland with our friends. (2)

9. our last game of netball is in december. (2)

10. when I grow up I want to be an artist, like picasso. (2)

BOB time!

FULL STOPS

Full stop (.) A punctuation mark used at the **end of a sentence** to show that it is finished. The full stop also gives the reader a chance to **pause** before reading the next sentence. The next sentence always starts with a **capital letter**.

On Saturday I went to the football to see Melbourne play. I was sad they lost.

A full stop is used at the end of a **single word sentence.** **Stop. Yes.**

A full stop is used when writing **times**, like **7.30** am or **4.00** pm.

A full stop is used for an **abbreviation**. An abbreviation is a short way of writing something, like **Sat.** for Saturday or **Feb.** for February.

A full stop is used for writing **amounts of money**, like **$2.50** or **$15.00**.

We practise

Look at the full stops in these sentences.

A ticket to the movie on Fri. at 6.30 pm costs $12.50.

Full stop for an abbreviation (Fri.), a time (6.30), an amount of money ($12.50) and the end of the sentence.

Please come to my party on Sat. 18th of Nov. at Lollipops.

Full stop for two abbreviations (Sat. and Nov.) and the end of the sentence.

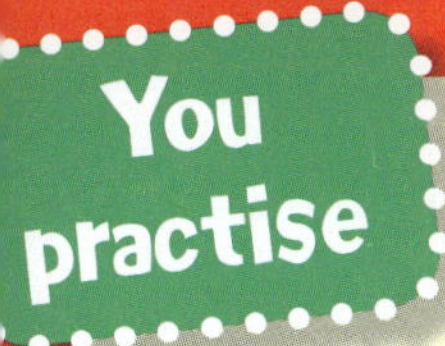

Add the eight missing full stops to this text.

On a clear and starry evening at about 6 00 pm, Tom rode his bike to his friend's house When he got there he was hot from riding so fast He and his friend Mike liked to play video games so they went to play on Mike's new Xbox Mike had saved up $300 00 to buy it It was really cool because you did not need a controller All you had to do was move your hands, your arms and legs or your body to make the character move

BOB time!

You practise

Add the seven missing full stops to this text.

The boys were having great fun playing a game They were so busy that they did not notice Mike's sister and her friend creeping up behind them The girls were both wearing black clothes and scary masks They screamed loudly The boys got such a fright that they screamed too and began to run out of the house into the rain Just as they were about to run out of the door, they saw that the monsters had taken off their masks and were laughing The boys did not know whether to be mad or to laugh

QUESTION MARKS

A **question** is a sentence that asks something that needs an answer.

A question starts with a capital letter and ends with a **question mark**.

Questions often start with the words:

How? Why? What? Where? Who?

Question:
Why was the broom late?
Answer:
Because it over swept.

We practise

Is this sentence a question?

What is your favourite animal.

Yes, so it must end with a question mark.

What is your favourite animal?

Is this sentence a question?

How do you make a banana split.

Yes, so it must end with a question mark.

How do you make a banana split?

We practise

You practise

Add a question mark or a full stop at the end of each sentence.

1 Today was cold, wet and windy

2 What would you like for lunch today

3 Do you know where my goggles are

4 The party was great fun

5 Would you like to go skateboarding after school

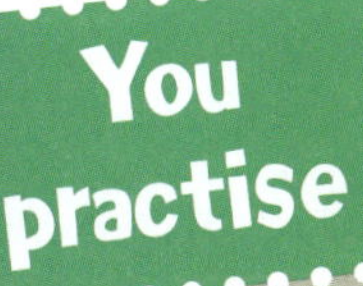

Add a question mark or a full stop at the end of each sentence.

6 Why don't you have your homework

7 What time does the train come

8 I love to play tennis

9 Where are you going for your holidays

10 Who has read all the Zac Power books

EXCLAMATION MARKS

An **exclamation** is a sentence that expresses a strong **feeling** or **emotion** about something, like joy, anger, excitement or surprise.

An exclamation starts with a capital letter and ends with an **exclamation mark**.

That was a great hockey match!

I love that!

Wow, look in the sky!

Run for your lives!

Help!

Ouch! That really hurt!

Oh my goodness!

We practise

Why do these sentences end in an exclamation mark?

It is snowing outside!

Emotion = joy, surprise

I would love to go to the party!

Emotion = joy, excitement

There's something moving under my bed!

Emotion = fear, surprise

I cannot believe how messy your room is!

Emotion = surprise, anger

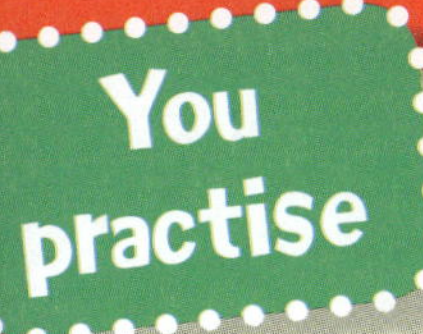

Add an exclamation mark or a question mark at the end of each sentence.

 1 I am starving – what time is lunch

 2 Oh no, the forecast is for rain today

 3 My new teacher is fantastic

 4 I have finished all my homework

 5 Do you know how to ride a horse

Add an exclamation mark or a question mark at the end of each sentence.

 6 Would you like to come over for a play

 7 I would love another lolly

 8 I've seen this *Toy Story* movie ten times

 9 It's my birthday tomorrow

 10 Have you finished your homework

UNIT 5

SENTENCE TYPES I

Statement

A sentence that tells a fact or an idea, which can be true or false.

We went to the park.

Emotion

A sentence that expresses emotions, or feelings, such as happiness or sadness.

I was **very sad** when my rabbit died.

Command

A sentence that makes a command, or an order, to do something.

Get in the car or you will be late.

Exclamation

A sentence that shows strong feelings or emotions, such as surprise, joy, anger or fear. An exclamation ends with an **exclamation mark**.

Hooray, it's Christmas tomorrow**!**

All sentence types start with a capital letter.

We can do it! (Exclamation)

What type of sentence is each of these – statement, emotion, command or exclamation?

We like fish and chips.

A **statement** because it tells a fact

I was excited to go swimming.

An **emotion** because it expresses an emotion – excitement

Slow down or you will fall.

A **command** because it is an order to do something – **slow down**

Wow! I can't believe you won the game!

An **exclamation** because it shows a strong feeling

You practise

What type of sentence is each of these – statement, emotion, command or exclamation?

1. My sister plays netball and football. ______________
2. I can't believe my eyes! ______________
3. Please come to the table for dinner now. ______________
4. Jeff was excited to go camping. ______________
5. Turn left at the roundabout. ______________

BOB time!

You practise

What type of sentence is each of these – statement, emotion, command or exclamation?

6. My favourite TV show is 'Ben 10'. ______________
7. There are 26 children in our class. ______________
8. Line up after the bell rings. ______________

9. Wow, the fireworks were amazing! ______________
10. I'm a bit nervous about going camping. ______________

BOB time!

NOUNS

Common noun

A word that names something. It can name a person, an animal, a place, a feeling, a thing or even an idea.

Proper noun

A word that names a particular person or a special place or thing. A proper noun starts with a **capital letter** to show that it is important.

horse = **common noun** – the name of a type of animal

Maria = **proper noun** – the name of a particular person

playground = **common noun** – the name of a place

Australia = **proper noun** – the name of an important place

embarrassed = **common noun** – the name of a type of feeling

Use a pronoun so that you don't repeat a noun too many times.

Pronoun A word that replaces a noun, such as **he**, **she** and **it**.

Toula peeled the **banana** and then **she** ate **it**.

Toula is a **noun.** **She** is a **pronoun** replacing the **noun Toula**.

Banana is a **noun**. **It** is a **pronoun** replacing the **noun banana**.

We practise

Some nouns have been circled in this text. Common nouns are green, proper nouns are yellow and pronouns are pink.

Once upon a time there was a school that was for children who liked to dance. It was called the Australian School of Dance. Peter wanted to go to this school because he loved to do rap dancing. Tina wanted to go to this school because she loved tap dancing. They hoped their dreams would come true.

UNIT 6

You practise

Some of the nouns in this text have been circled. Colour in each circle.
Use Yellow for proper nouns,
Green for common nouns and Pink for pronouns.

There was once a hare named Harry who thought he was a very good runner. So good, that he would boast that he could beat anyone. One day he made a challenge. "I can beat anyone in a race and I challenge anyone to try. A tortoise named Tessa said, "I can beat you." Harry the hare laughed and they agreed to race on Saturday in his home town of Darwin. The race started and Harry the hare was a long way in the lead. He decided to have a rest for a little while. He fell asleep.

BOB time!

You practise

Some of the nouns in this text have been circled. Colour in each circle.
Use Yellow for proper nouns,
Green for common nouns and Pink for pronouns.

Tessa the tortoise kept plodding along and soon she passed the sleeping hare. Harry the hare woke up just in time to see Tessa the tortoise cross the finishing line. Harry was sad and knew that he had been bragging and that he should have tried harder. Tessa was happy she had worked hard and had proven that slow and steady wins the race.

BOB time!

ADJECTIVES

Adjective

A word that describes a noun.

The **table** was **heavy**.

noun — adjective

It was a **rainy** **day**.

adjective — noun

Adjectives make your writing more interesting

We practise

There are eight adjectives circled in this text. Remember that an adjective describes a noun.

Our family went to the airport to watch all the big aeroplanes fly. We saw some fast jets. We saw some enormous aeroplanes that are called jumbo jets. We saw a small seaplane that can land on water. We saw a military plane that is used by the army. We had a great day watching all the amazing planes take off and land.

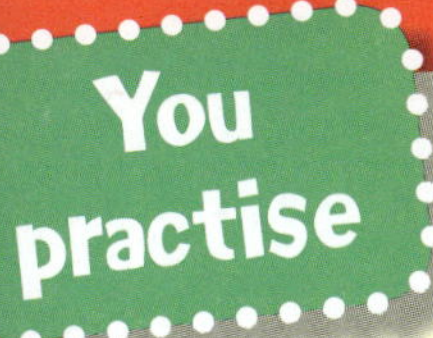

Circle ten adjectives in this list of words.

beautiful snail flat embarrassed bicycle

man angry girl short big

lady helpful loud happy beach

tall house chair school bird

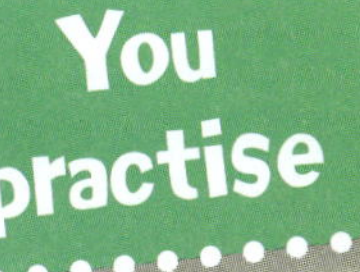

Circle the adjective in each sentence.
Remember that an adjective describes a noun.

The hot water spilled out of the bath.

The long tail of the horse swished at the flies.

A red car went speeding down the road.

A mysterious spaceship flashed across the sky.

The old man sat down to rest.

CONCRETE AND ABSTRACT NOUNS

Concrete noun

A noun that names people, places and things. A concrete noun is something that you can **see**, **touch**, **hear**, **taste** or **smell**.

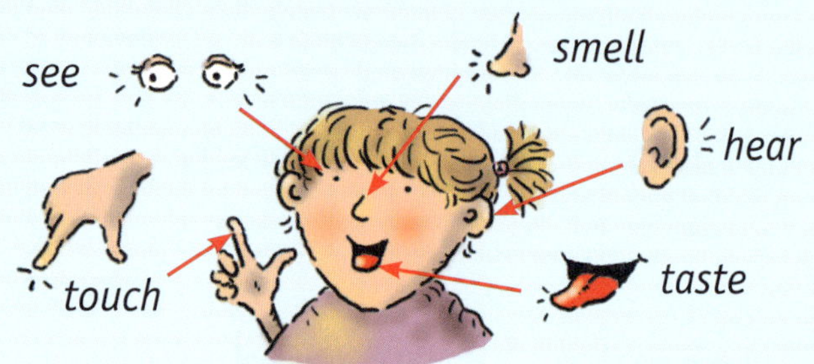

student	you can **see**, **touch** and **hear** a student
bread	you can **see**, **touch**, **taste** and **smell** bread
dog	you can **see**, **touch**, **smell** and **hear** a dog
pencil	you can **see** and **touch** a pencil
bus	you can **see**, **touch** and **hear** a bus

Abstract noun

A noun that names emotions and ideas you **cannot** use your five senses with.

You cannot **see** them.

You cannot **hear** them.

You cannot **smell** them.

You cannot **taste** them.

You cannot **touch** them.

curiosity **sadness** **fear**
bravery **hate**
joy **love** **luck**
sleep **pain**

How do you know if a noun is abstract or concrete?

Sue received an award for **bravery**.

Can you see, hear, smell, taste or touch **bravery**?

No = **abstract noun**

The **monkey** swung in the tree.

Can you see, hear, smell, taste or touch a **monkey**?

Yes = **concrete noun**

You practise Circle ten concrete nouns in this story.

When I woke up I was hungry after a long sleep. I needed some breakfast. I poured some juice into a glass and put two pieces of bread into the toaster. I got a big surprise when the toast popped out of the toaster! I spread butter and honey on my toast. I drank the juice, ate the toast and then I enjoyed a banana. After breakfast I got dressed in my uniform and with pride I tied my own shoelaces. With any luck, I would be early for school today so I could meet my friends and play a game of marbles before the bell. I didn't want to be late.

BOB time!

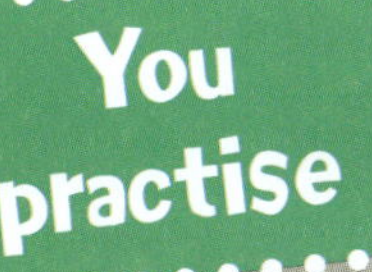

Now circle four abstract nouns in the story.

When I woke up I was hungry after a long sleep. I needed some breakfast. I poured some juice into a glass and put two pieces of bread into the toaster. I got a big surprise when the toast popped out of the toaster! I spread butter and honey on my toast. I drank the juice, ate the toast and then I enjoyed a banana. After breakfast I got dressed in my uniform and with pride I tied my own shoelaces. With any luck, I would be early for school today so I could meet my friends and play a game of marbles before the bell. I didn't want to be late.

BOB time!

UNIT 9

VERBS AND ADVERBS

Verb

A 'doing' word.

A verb shows action.

The fox **ran** across the field.

ran = action = **verb**

The monkey **climbed** the tree.

climbed = action = **verb**

Frances **walked** to school.

walked = action = **verb**

Hannah **swam** in the pool.

swam = action = **verb**

Adverb

A word that adds meaning to a verb or describes 'how' an action is done.

walking slowly

The adverb **slowly** adds meaning to or describes the verb **walking.**

Adverbs usually end in **ly** or **ily**.
proudly, lazily, bravely, noisily

We practise

The verb is underlined and the adverb is circled in each sentence.

Hint: the adverb likes to sit next to the verb.

We <u>smiled</u> (happily) when we saw our friends.

The dog <u>growled</u> (loudly) at the cat.

She (easily) <u>jumped</u> over the fence.

Matt (quickly) <u>finished</u> his homework.

You practise

Underline one verb and circle one adverb in each sentence.

1. She carefully crossed the road.

2. Mrs Brown spoke kindly to the children.

3. Can you please work quietly?

4. The jet flew speedily across the sky.

5. Mary shouted crossly at her dog to come back.

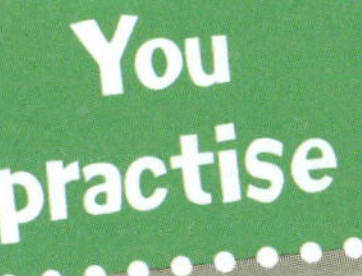

Underline one verb and circle one adverb in each sentence.

6. Collingwood played strongly against Melbourne.

7. Tamir quickly ate his lunch so he could go and play.

8. On Thursday it rained heavily all afternoon.

9. The stars twinkled brightly in the sky that night.

10. The witch laughed wickedly.

BOB time!

SYNONYMS

Synonyms are similar.

Synonym

A word that has a **similar** meaning to another word.

happy	–	*cheerful*
shout	–	*yell*
tired	–	*weary*
hard	–	*difficult*

A line matches each word with its synonym. Both words have a similar meaning.

We practise

chilly	sketch
bravery	frighten
draw	cool
scare	skinny
thin	courage

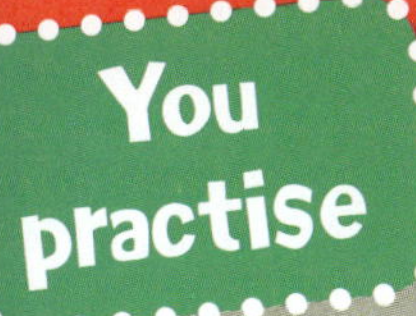

Draw a line to match each word with its synonym.

many — great

good — lots

beautiful — high

tall — close

near — pretty

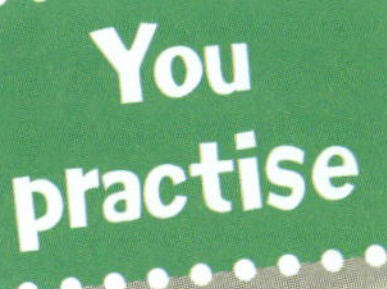

Draw a line to match each word with its synonym.

brave — furious

big — ache

clever — large

mad — smart

pain — fearless

ANTONYMS

Antonym
A word that has the **opposite** meaning to another word.

happy	–	*sad*
fast	–	*slow*
high	–	*low*
inside	–	*outside*

We practise

A line matches each word with its antonym. Both words have the opposite meaning.

black	cold
hot	short
in	white
long	narrow
wide	out

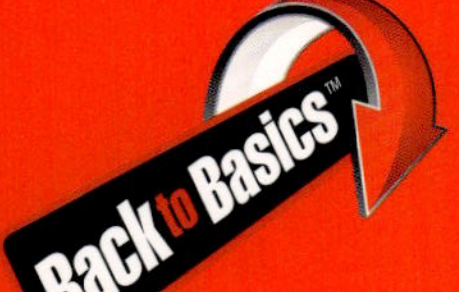

PARTS OF SPEECH

YEAR 2

PARTS OF SPEECH

YEAR 2

PARTS OF SPEECH

YEAR 2

PARTS OF SPEECH

YEAR 2

PARTS OF SPEECH

YEAR 2

PARTS OF SPEECH

YEAR 2

PARTS OF SPEECH

YEAR 2

PARTS OF SPEECH

YEAR 2

PARTS OF SPEECH

YEAR 2

PARTS OF SPEECH

YEAR 2

PARTS OF SPEECH

YEAR 2

PARTS OF SPEECH

YEAR 2

Noun	Adjective	Verb
Pronoun	Conjunction	Adverb
chair	sticky	table
went	his	sadly

they	and	car
walking	mouse	fast
she	quietly	run
brown	but	soft

Back to Basics™

PARTS OF SPEECH

YEAR 2

PARTS OF SPEECH

YEAR 2

PARTS OF SPEECH

YEAR 2

PARTS OF SPEECH

YEAR 2

PARTS OF SPEECH

YEAR 2

PARTS OF SPEECH

YEAR 2

PARTS OF SPEECH

YEAR 2

PARTS OF SPEECH

YEAR 2

PARTS OF SPEECH

YEAR 2

PARTS OF SPEECH

YEAR 2

PARTS OF SPEECH

YEAR 2

PARTS OF SPEECH

YEAR 2

You practise

Draw a line to match each word with its antonym.

many | ugly

good | far

beautiful | bad

tall | few

5 near | short

You practise

Draw a line to match each word with its antonym.

kind | quiet

fat | old

under | cruel

loud | over

young | thin

COMMAS

Comma

,

A punctuation mark that shows the reader **when to pause** when reading a sentence. This helps the reader to understand the sentence.

I walked to the park near my house, taking a shortcut through the bush.

A comma is also used to **separate items in a list**.

I packed my school bag with my lunch, a drink, my homework and a hat.

We practise

The commas in these sentences separate items in a list or tell the reader when to pause.

After the game was over, we went home to celebrate.

Jonah travelled to Perth, Darwin, Brisbane, Sydney and Melbourne.

It was a cold and clear night, stars twinkling above.

Maria put a hockey stick, a spare ball, her mouth guard and a water bottle into her sports bag.

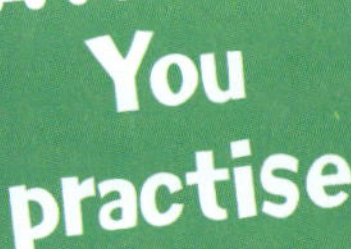

For each sentence, add a comma to tell the reader when to pause or to separate items in a list.

1 I went fishing off the pier using yabbies for bait.

2 For lunch Joey had a sandwich an apple a drink and some chips.

3 We went shopping and I bought some shoes a t-shirt a pair of shorts and a jumper.

4 In our vegetable garden we are growing tomatoes my favourite food!

5 At the zoo we saw fierce lions growly bears cute koalas and cheeky monkeys!

You practise

For each sentence, add a comma to tell the reader when to pause or to separate items in a list.

6 My ice-cream has vanilla chocolate and mint.

7 At her friend's house Jane played in the swimming pool.

8 To play soccer you need a ball boots and shin guards.

9 It was a cold day so we could not go to the beach.

10 If I had a million dollars I would buy a house a car a motorbike and a big TV!

BOB time!

UNIT 13

COMPOUND SENTENCES

Compound sentence

A sentence that has two parts.

Each part *could* be a short sentence on its own.

The puppy was cute and his fur was black with a white spot.

1st part: The puppy was cute

2nd part: his fur was black with a white spot.

Conjunction

A joining word. A conjunction **joins** the two parts of a sentence.

The puppy was cute **and** his fur was black with a white spot.

↑ conjunction

Conjunctions are joining words, such as **and, but, because, or, nor, for, so** and **yet.**

Compound means **two parts together.**

We practise

The conjunction is circled in these compound sentences.

The sun shone brightly that morning (and) the birds began to sing.

The movie was over (so) we went to get some lunch.

The bell rang loudly (because) it was time to go into school.

She plays the piano well (yet) she can't read music.

You practise

Use a conjunction from the box to complete each compound sentence.

but and because so yet

1. My sister and I went to the park __________ climbed the trees.
2. My dad rides his bike to work __________ he drives when it's raining.
3. Art is my favourite subject at school __________ I love to paint.
4. We were late for the movie __________ we had to go to the next one.
5. The sky was grey __________ it was a warm day.

BOB time!

You practise

Use a conjunction from the box to complete each compound sentence.

but because then so and

6. I watch the footy __________ I can cheer for the mighty Magpies!
7. The old man had slept well __________ he was still tired.
8. A goat got into the garden __________ it ate all our vegetables!
9. We rode our horses along the beach __________ we took the horses swimming.
10. My mum picked me up early __________ I was sick.

BOB time!

PREFIXES AND SUFFIXES

Prefix A group of letters added to the **front** of a word to make a new word. Often a prefix makes a word with the opposite meaning.

Add the prefix **dis** to **appear** to make a new word – **dis**appear.
Add the prefix **un** to **plug** to make a new word – **un**plug.
Add the prefix **re** to **do** to make a new word – **re**do.

Unbelievable!

Suffix A group of letters added to the **end** of a word to make a new word.

Add the suffix **less** to **pain** to make a new word – pain**less**.
Add the suffix **ful** to **wonder** to make a new word – wonder**ful**.
Add the suffix **ly** to **love** to make a new word – love**ly**.

Don't be careless!

We practise

A prefix has been added to each word to make a new word.

do + **un** = **un**do ✔
open + **re** = **re**open ✔

A suffix has been added to each word to make a new word.

quick + **ly** = quick**ly** ✔
care + **less** = care**less** ✔

You practise

Use the prefixes in the box to make new words.

dis	im	in	anti	un

 1 ________ happy

 2 ________ obey

 3 ________ clockwise

 4 ________ visible

 5 ________ possible

BOB time!

You practise

Use the suffixes in the box to make new words.

less	ful	ly	ing	ness

 6 hand ________

 7 shy ________

 8 love ________

 9 play ________

 10 care ________

HOMOPHONES

Homophone

A word that **sounds the same** as another word, but has a **different spelling** and **different meaning**.

flower		flour	
see		sea	
hair	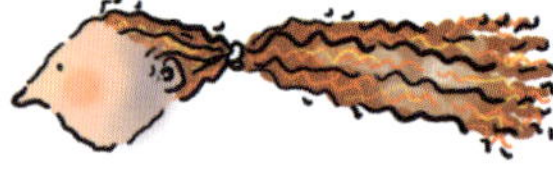	hare	
pear		pair	

You can use a dictionary to check the meaning of a word.

We practise

The homophone with the correct meaning is circled in each sentence.

Can you please paw / (pour) me a glass of milk?

We had fairy floss at the (fair) / fare.

The sky was a beautiful bright blew / (blue.)

The boat's sale / (sail) flapped in the wind.

You practise

Circle the correct homophone in each sentence.

1 Can I please have **too** / **two** apples?

2 When we go to the beach we swim in the **see** / **sea**.

3 Did you **hear** / **here** what I said?

4 The **witch** / **which** flew on her broom.

5 I had to wait two **ours** / **hours** to see the dentist.

BOB time!

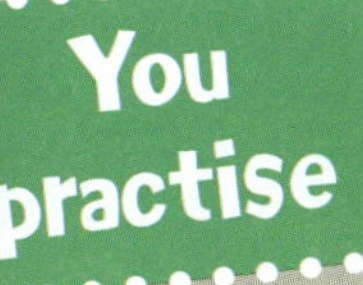

Circle the correct homophone in each sentence.

6 I **ate** / **eight** cupcakes.

7 I have **won** / **one** lolly left to eat.

8 The **plain** / **plane** flew high in the sky.

9 Your ball is over **their** / **there** in the sand.

10 When we go to the zoo I want to see a polar **bare** / **bear**.

BOB time!

SENTENCE TYPES 2

Do you remember?

Statement

We went to the river.

This is a statement because it tells a fact, which can be true or false.

Emotion

I was very **happy** when the sun shone.

This sentence expresses the **emotion** of happiness.

Command

Hurry, come inside for lunch.

This is a command because it makes an order.

Exclamation

Your work is excellent!

This is an exclamation because it shows a strong feeling and it ends in an **exclamation mark**.

We practise

How do you know if a sentence is a statement, emotion, command or exclamation?

You are amazing!	An **exclamation** because it shows a strong feeling
It's sad that your goldfish died.	An **emotion** because it expresses an emotion – sadness
We will arrive on Tuesday.	A **statement** because it tells a fact
Take the dog outside please.	A **command** because it makes an order to do something – take

You practise

What type of sentence is each of these – statement, emotion, command or exclamation?

1. That is the coolest car I've ever seen! ____________________

2. Put that down. ____________________

3. Ava and Zola were friends at school. ____________________

4. James was nervous about starting school. ____________________

5. Redback spiders are very dangerous. ____________________

BOB time!

You practise

What type of sentence is each of these – statement, emotion, command or exclamation?

6. Alex was happy to get a new puppy. ____________________

7. Wow, that movie was awesome! ____________________

8. Cathy Freeman won a gold medal at the Sydney Olympic Games in 2000. ____________________

9. I will jump for joy if I win a prize. ____________________

10. Paula was hurt so she couldn't play netball. ____________________

BOB time!

PUNCTUATION

Do you remember?

Capital letter	**ABC**	Sentences and proper nouns start with a capital letter.
Full stop	**.**	Sentences end with a full stop.
Question mark	**?**	Questions end with a question mark.
Exclamation mark	**!**	Exclamations end with an exclamation mark.
Comma	**,**	Shows the reader when to pause and separates items in a list.

We practise

The punctuation is highlighted in this text.

Today is my birthday and I will have a special dinner with my family**.** **W**e will have a birthday cake and then I will be able to open my birthday presents**.** **I** can't wait**!** **M**y mother**,** father**,** sister**,** grandma and grandpa will all sing '**H**appy **B**irthday'**.** **W**ould you like to come too**?**

You practise

Rewrite these sentences, adding the correct punctuation.

1 what's that noise ______________________

2 Help it's a monster ______________________

3 you left mud on the stairs carpet and rug

____

4 the pirate dug and dug to find the treasure

____

5 are you hungry yet ______________________

BOB time!

You practise

Rewrite these sentences, adding the correct punctuation.

6 did you see sharks swimming in the sea

____

7 santa comes the night before christmas

____

8 ouch that hurt ______________________

9 be quiet ______________________

10 we bought apples oranges pears and grapes

____

BOB time!

PARTS OF SPEECH

Common noun A word that names something – a person, an animal, a place, a feeling, a thing or even an idea.

Proper noun A word that names a particular person or a special place or thing. It starts with a capital letter to show that it is important.
Mount Everest, Elvis Presley, Monday

Concrete noun A word that names people, places and things that you can see, touch, hear, taste or smell.
bread, dog, pencil, chair

Abstract noun A word that names emotions, feelings or ideas that you cannot see, touch, hear, taste or smell. luck, love, sleep

Pronoun A word that replaces a noun. he, she, it

Adjective A word that describes a noun. **hard** chair

Verb A 'doing' word, a word that shows action. run, jump, hop, fly

Adverb A word that adds meaning to a verb or describes 'how' the action is done. **quickly** run

Do you remember?

The parts of speech in this text are recorded in the table below.

In the Pacific Ocean I saw a huge whale. I was in my uncle's boat, far from the beach. I felt a rush of excitement. "Look at him!" I called loudly, because I could hardly believe my eyes. Then I quickly grabbed my camera to take a photo.

proper noun	Pacific Ocean
common noun	boat, beach, whale, camera, eyes, excitement
concrete noun	boat, beach, whale, camera, eyes
abstract noun	excitement
pronoun	I, him
adjective	huge
verb	saw, called, grabbed
adverb	loudly, quickly

We practise

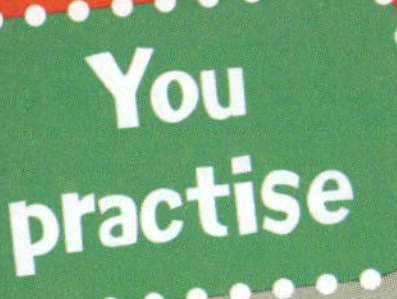

Find these parts of speech in the following text.

proper noun	
common noun	
concrete noun	
abstract noun	
pronoun	
adjective	
verb	
adverb	

Barry had a very good life. He had good food, a big, soft bed, and the Hazell family to look after him. One morning Barry woke up from a long sleep. "I'm hungry!" he said. He went down to the kitchen but everyone in the Hazell family was still asleep. Barry went outside and stomped down the street. On the footpath he saw an ice-cream. He happily ate it. "Gulp!" Down went the ice-cream. Next, Barry headed for the park. There he found a pair of shoes. "Gulp!" Down they went too. "Mmmm, yum!" said Barry. He was feeling very full as he plodded over to a video store. There he saw some tasty video games. "Gulp! Gulp! Gulp!" Barry swallowed *Let's Dance* and *Wii Fit* whole. "Wow! It must be time to go home," said Barry. He ran back home and up the stairs to his soft bed. "Breakfast! Time for breakfast, Barry!" called Mrs Hazell. "I don't feel very well, I have a pain in my tummy," groaned Barry. "It must have been something I ate. Burp!"

BOB time!

GRAMMAR

Read this story and then complete the tables on the next page.

The Ugly Duckling

Once upon a time a Mother Duck laid six eggs, but when the eggs hatched there were seven ducklings. The seventh duckling had grey feathers and was bigger than all the others. The Mother Duck was surprised that the seventh duckling was so ugly and ate more than the others.

The poor ugly duckling became more and more unhappy. His brothers and sisters didn't want to play with him, he was so clumsy, and all the farmyard folks simply laughed at him. He felt sad.

One day, he ran away. He saw some other birds and he asked them if they knew any ducklings that looked like him. But no one did. Some even told him to go away!

He ran further and further away. He found a pond where there was lots of food. One day, he saw some birds flying across the sky. They had long necks, yellow beaks and large wings. They were flying south for the winter. The ugly duckling thought they were the most beautiful birds he had ever seen.

Winter came and a farmer found the ugly duckling and took him home so his children could look after him. The children were kind to him.

When spring came the farmer took the ugly duckling to the pond. The ugly duckling saw his reflection in the water. He looked just like the beautiful birds with long necks, yellow beaks and large wings that had flown south for the winter.

Suddenly, those very same birds landed in the pond. The ugly duckling realised he was just like them and he soon made friends.

One day, he saw some ducks and the youngest one said, "Look at that swan! He is beautiful."

The ugly duckling had never felt such happiness!

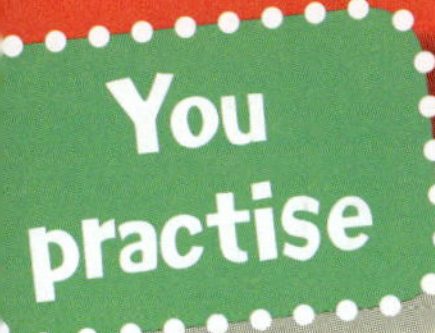

The Ugly Duckling

Find a word from the story that is a ...	
Proper noun	
Common noun	
Concrete noun	
Abstract noun	
Pronoun	
Adjective	
Verb	
Adverb	

BOB time!

Find one of each of these sentence types in the story.
Statement
Exclamation
Emotion
Command

BOB time!

PUNCTUATION TEST 1

My visit to a volcano

In the Sept. holidays I visited Hawaii and went on a special tour that took me very close to a real, active volcano.

The tour cost $20.00 and started at 10.30 am and went all day until 5.00 pm. I had to take my hat, a drink and my lunch with me.

I learnt that the solid ground we walk on is part of the Earth's crust. Below the crust is a hot layer of molten rock (liquid rock) called magma. Did you know that when the magma explodes through an opening in the Earth's crust, a volcano erupts?

I also learnt that a volcano is one of nature's most frightening and fantastic events. Volcanoes can have a huge effect on the Earth. They can bury a town or they can create a mountain. Volcanoes can change the world!

Circle one of each of these in the text.

Capital letter to begin a sentence	/1
Capital letter to begin a proper noun	/1
Full stop to end a sentence	/1
Full stop to end an abbreviation	/1
Full stop in a time	/1
Full stop in an amount of money	/1
Comma to show a pause in a sentence	/1
Comma to separate items in a list	/1
Question mark	/1
Exclamation mark	/1
Total	**/10**

PUNCTUATION TEST 2

My walking fish

When my Mum said that I could have a pet, I decided to get a fish. Mum said we could go to the pet shop after school on Fri. at 3.30 pm.

At the pet shop I found exactly the fish I wanted. Did you know there is a fish that has legs? This fish is called an axolotl (you say it axo-lot-il).

Axolotls are also sometimes called Mexican walking fish. They look a bit like a tadpole and have a long tail, four legs, a fin and a pair of gills on their head. Axolotls can live as long as 25 years!

My axolotl cost $20.50. I also had to buy some food, a tank, gravel and some rocks.

If you are looking for a different pet, then you should get an axolotl.

Circle one of each of these in the text.

Capital letter to begin a sentence	/1
Proper noun	/1
Full stop to end a sentence	/1
Full stop to end an abbreviation	/1
Full stop in a time	/1
Full stop in an amount of money	/1
Comma to show a pause in a sentence	/1
Comma to separate items in a list	/1
Question mark	/1
Exclamation mark	/1
Total	**/10**

GRAMMAR TEST 1

The Heebie Jeebie

"Boo!" said Spook with a grin. Olivia almost leapt through the ceiling with fright. Spook held out one of his hands. Olivia sank under her bed covers and started shaking.

"What ... what ... are you?" she asked. Olivia was scared and trembling so much she could hardly get her words out.

"His name is Spook. He is part of the Night Beastie Security Patrol," said Toby with a smile. "There has been a report from a Jeepers Creeper about an unknown beastie, known as a Heebie Jeebie, in the house." Olivia curled deeper under her covers.

"I was wondering if you have seen or heard anything that might help us find it," said Spook.

"This can't be real ..." muttered Olivia as she shook.

Suddenly Lurk, part of the Night Beastie Security Patrol, yelled, "Come quickly! I've netted the Heebie Jeebie!"

"Hey! That's not a Heebie Jeebie!" cried Toby. "That is a stuffed toy. My grandma made it for me when I was little."

By Lisa Thompson

Label one of each of these in the text.

Proper noun	PN	/1
Common noun	C	/1
Concrete noun	CN	/1
Abstract noun	AN	/1
Pronouns	P	/1
Adjective	A	/1
Verb	V	/1
Adverb	AV	/1

Circle one of each of these in the text.

Synonym for **smile**	/1
Antonym for **whispered**	/1
Total	**/10**

GRAMMAR TEST 2

The secret cave

Every year my family goes to the beach for a holiday. I remember one year when my sister and I found a secret cave.

We were tired of playing in the sea so we decided to go exploring. We soon found a big cave. We carefully stepped in and then suddenly felt very cold. It was dark and spooky and there was a very unpleasant smell.

We bravely walked deeper inside and then my sister screamed. She slowly pointed at the wet, slimy wall, but I could not see anything. We were both unable to move. We nervously looked at each other and then quickly ran out of the cave, both screaming.

Afterwards, when we were safely at home, we decided to go back the next day.

Label one of each of these in the text.

Pronoun	P	/1
Adjective	A	/1
Verb	V	/1
Adverb	AV	/1
Conjunction	C	/1

Circle one of each of these in the text.

Synonym for **chilly**	/1
Antonym for **light**	/1
Prefix **un**	/1
Suffix **ing**	/1
Homophone for **sea**	/1
Total	**/10**

ANSWERS

Unit 1

1 **T**oday is **M**onday and it is a school day.
2 **W**atch out for that truck!
3 **H**ave you seen the movie called *Shrek*?
4 **M**r **W**alker is our teacher at school this year.
5 **O**ur dog **B**en carried the ball in his mouth.
6 **O**n **S**aturdays **T**im loves to watch the football.
7 **M**y friends **S**ophie and **A**nna are coming for a sleepover.
8 **W**e went on a holiday to **Q**ueensland with our friends.
9 **O**ur last game of netball is in **D**ecember.
10 **W**hen I grow up I want to be an artist, like **P**icasso.

Unit 2

On a clear and starry evening at about 6.00 pm, Tom rode his bike to his friend's house. When he got there he was hot from riding so fast. Tom and his friend Mike liked to play video games so they played on Mike's new Xbox. Mike had saved up $300.00 to buy it. It was really cool because you did not need a controller. All you had to do was move your hands, your arms and legs or your body to make the character move.

The boys were having great fun playing a game. They were so busy that they did not notice Mike's sister and her friend creeping up behind them. The girls were both wearing black clothes and scary masks. They screamed loudly. The boys got such a fright that they screamed too and began to run out of the house into the rain. Just as they were about to run out of the door, they saw that the monsters had taken off their masks and were laughing. The boys did not know whether to be mad or to laugh.

Unit 3

1 Today was cold, wet and windy.
2 What would you like for lunch today?
3 Do you know where my goggles are?
4 The party was great fun.
5 Would you like to go skateboarding after school?
6 Why don't you have your homework?
7 What time does the train come?
8 I love to play tennis.
9 Where are you going for your holidays?
10 Who has read all the Zac Power books?

Unit 4

1 I am starving – what time is lunch?
2 Oh no, the forecast is for rain today!
3 My new teacher is fantastic!
4 I have finished all my homework!
5 Do you know how to ride a horse?
6 Would you like to come over for a play?
7 I would love another lolly!
8 I've seen this *Toy Story* movie ten times!
9 It's my birthday tomorrow!
10 Have you finished your homework?

Unit 5

1 statement
2 exclamation
3 command
4 emotion
5 command
6 statement
7 statement
8 command
9 exclamation
10 emotion

Unit 6

Proper nouns: Harry, Tessa, Saturday, Darwin
Common nouns: hare, runner, day, race, tortoise
Pronouns: he, I, they, she

Unit 7

beautiful, flat, embarrassed, angry, short, big, helpful, loud, happy, tall

1 hot
2 long
3 red
4 mysterious
5 old

Unit 8

Concrete nouns: breakfast, juice, glass, bread, toast, toaster, butter, honey, banana, uniform, shoelaces, school, friends, game, marbles, bell
Abstract nouns: sleep, pride, luck, surprise

Unit 9

1 **Verb**: crossed **Adverb**: carefully
2 **Verb**: spoke: **Adverb**: kindly
3 **Verb**: work **Adverb**: quietly
4 **Verb**: flew **Adverb**: speedily
5 **Verb**: shouted **Adverb**: crossly
6 **Verb**: played **Adverb**: strongly
7 **Verb**: ate **Adverb**: quickly
8 **Verb**: rained **Adverb**: heavily
9 **Verb**: twinkled **Adverb**: brightly
10 **Verb**: laughed **Adverb**: wickedly

Unit 10

1 many – lots
2 good – great
3 beautiful – pretty
4 tall – high
5 near – close
6 brave – fearless
7 big – large
8 clever – smart
9 mad – furious
10 pain – ache

ANSWERS

Unit 11

1 many – few
2 good – bad
3 beautiful – ugly
4 tall – short
5 near – far
6 kind – cruel
7 fat – thin
8 under – over
9 loud – quiet
10 young – old

Unit 12

1 I went fishing off the pier, using yabbies for bait.
2 For lunch Joey had a sandwich, an apple, a drink and some chips.
3 We went shopping and I bought some shoes, a t-shirt, a pair of shorts and a jumper.
4 In our vegetable garden we are growing tomatoes, my favourite food!
5 At the zoo we saw fierce lions, growly bears, cute koalas and very cheeky monkeys!
6 My ice-cream has vanilla, chocolate and mint.
7 At her friend's house, Jane played in the swimming pool.
8 To play soccer you need a ball, soccer boots and shin guards.
9 It was a cold day, so we could not go to the beach.
10 If I had a million dollars, I would buy a house, a car, a motorbike and a big TV!

Unit 13

1 and
2 but
3 because
4 so
5 yet
6 so
7 but
8 and
9 then
10 because

Unit 14

1 unhappy
2 disobey
3 anticlockwise
4 invisible
5 impossible
6 handful / handing
7 shyness / shyly / shying
8 lovely / loveless
9 playful / playing
10 careless / careful

Unit 15

1 two
2 sea
3 hear
4 witch
5 hours
6 ate
7 one
8 plane
9 there
10 bear

Unit 16

1 exclamation
2 command
3 statement
4 emotion
5 statement
6 emotion
7 exclamation
8 statement
9 emotion
10 statement

Unit 17

1 **W**hat's that noise**?**
2 **H**elp, it's a monster**!**
3 **Y**ou left mud on the stairs, carpet and the rug**!** (or **.**)
4 **T**he pirate dug and dug to find the treasure**.**
5 **A**re you hungry yet**?**
6 **D**id you see sharks swimming in the sea**?**
7 **S**anta comes the night before **C**hristmas**.**
8 **O**uch, that hurt**!**
9 **B**e quiet**!** (or **.**)
10 **W**e bought apples, oranges, pears and grapes**.**

Unit 18

Answers will vary.

Proper nouns	Barry, Hazell, *Let's Dance*, *Wii Fit*, Mrs Hazell
Common nouns	food, bed, morning, kitchen, street, footpath, ice-cream, park, shoes, store, video games, home, stairs, breakfast, tummy
Concrete nouns	food, bed, kitchen, street, footpath, ice-cream, park, shoes, store, video games, home, stairs, breakfast
Abstract nouns	sleep, pain, life, morning
Pronouns	he, everyone, it, they, him, I, something
Adjectives	good, big, soft, hungry, asleep, pair, full, tasty
Verbs	woke up, went, stomped, saw, ate, headed, found, said, gulp, plodded, swallowed, ran, groaned, called, go, feel, look after
Adverbs	happily, back

ANSWERS

Unit 19
Answers will vary.

Proper noun	Mother Duck
Common nouns	mother duck, eggs, ducklings, day, feathers, brothers, sisters, folks, birds, pond, food, sky, necks, beaks, wings, winter, farmer, home, spring, reflection, water, children, friends, swan, ducks
Concrete noun	mother duck, eggs, ducklings, feathers, brothers, sisters, folks, birds, pond, food, sky, necks, beaks, wings, farmer, home, reflection, water, children, friends, swan, ducks
Abstract noun	winter, spring, day, happiness
Pronoun	it, he, him, they, them
Adjective	six, seven, extra, grey, bigger, seventh, ugly, poor, unhappy, surprised, clumsy, farmyard, sad, long, yellow, large, beautiful, south, kind, youngest
Verb	laid, hatched, ate, play, laughed, felt, ran, saw, asked, told, found, flying, seen, took, look after, came, looked, landed, realised, made, said
Adverb	quickly, simply, away, further, ever, soon
Statement Once upon a time a Mother Duck laid six eggs.	
Exclamation Look at that swan!	
Emotion The poor ugly duckling became more and more unhappy.	
Command Some even told him to go away!	

Unit 20
Punctuation Test 1
Answers will vary.
Capital letter to begin a sentence : **I**n
Capital letter to begin a proper noun: **H**awaii, **E**arth
Full stop to end a sentence: ... active volcano**.**
Full stop to end an abbreviation: Sept**.**
Full stop in a time: 10**.**30 am, 5**.**00 pm
Full stop in an amount of money: $20**.**00
Comma to show a pause in a sentence: ... crust**,** a volcano erupts?
Comma to separate items in a list: I had to take my hat**,** a drink and my lunch with me.
Question mark: ... volcano erupts**?**
Exclamation mark: Volcanoes can change the world**!**

Punctuation Test 2
Answers will vary.
Capital letter to begin a sentence: **W**hen, **A**t, **M**y
Capital letter to begin a proper noun: **M**um, **M**exican
Full stop to end a sentence: ... the fish I wanted**.**
Full stop to end an abbreviation: Fri**.**
Full stop in a time: 3**.**30 pm
Full stop in an amount of money: $20**.**50
Comma to show a pause in a sentence: ... have a pet**,** I decided to get a fish.
Comma to separate items in a list: ... a long tail**,** four legs**,** a fin and a pair of gills
Question mark: ... has legs**?**
Exclamation mark: ... as 25 years**!**

Grammar Test 1
Answers will vary.
Proper nouns: Spook, Olivia, Toby, Night Beastie Security Patrol, Jeepers Creeper, Heebie Jeebie, Lurk
Common nouns: grin, ceiling, hands, bed covers, words, smile, report, beastie, house, toy, grandma,
Concrete nouns: grin, ceiling, hands, bed covers, smile, beastie, house, toy, grandma
Abstract noun: fright
Pronouns: his, she, it, he, her, I, us, me, you
Adjectives: scared, trembling, unknown, stuffed, little
Verbs: said, leapt, held, sank, shaking, asked, get, curled, wondering, seen, heard, help, find, muttered, shook, yelled, come, netted, cried, made
Adverbs: almost, under, hardly, deeper, quickly
Synonym for the word **smile** = grin
Antonym for the word **whispered** = yelled

Grammar Test 2
Answers will vary.
Pronouns: we, I, she
Adjectives: secret, dark, spooky, unpleasant, big, wet, slimy
Verbs: goes, remember, found, tired, decided, exploring, walked, stepped, felt, screamed, pointed, see, looked, ran, screaming
Adverbs: carefully, suddenly, bravely, slowly, nervously, quickly, afterwards, safely
Conjunctions: and, but, so
Synonym for **chilly:** cold
Antonym for **light**: dark
Prefix **un:** unable, unpleasant
Suffix **ing:** playing, exploring, screaming
Homophone for **see:** sea

Game card answers
Nouns: chair, table, car, mouse
Adjectives: sticky, fast, brown, soft
Verbs: went, walking, run
Pronouns: his, they, she
Conjunctions: and, but
Adverbs: sadly, quietly